W9-AGW-178

BECOMING AN
AMERICAN CITIZEN

by Clara MacCarald

Content Consultant
Richard Bell
Associate Professor, Department of History
University of Maryland

Core Library

An Imprint of Abdo Publishing
abdopublishing.com

abdopublishing.com

Published by Abdo Publishing, a division of ABDO, PO Box 398166, Minneapolis, Minnesota 55439. Copyright © 2017 by Abdo Consulting Group, Inc. International copyrights reserved in all countries. No part of this book may be reproduced in any form without written permission from the publisher. Core Library™ is a trademark and logo of Abdo Publishing.

Printed in the United States of America, North Mankato, Minnesota
042016
092016

Cover Photo: Ross D. Franklin/AP Images
Interior Photos: Ross D. Franklin/AP Images, 1; Chris Parypa Photography/Shutterstock Images, 4, 43; Ian Shaw/Alamy, 6; Library of Congress, 9; Red Line Editorial, 10, 41; Library of Congress, 12; Mark Lennihan/AP Images, 18; Spencer Platt/Getty Images, 21; Epoxydude/fstop/Corbis, 24, 45; Michael S. Williamson/The Washington Post/Getty Images, 28; John Moore/Getty Images, 30, 36; Mark Boster/Los Angeles Times/Getty Images, 33; Mark Lennihan/AP Images, 38

Editor: Sharon F. Doorasamy
Series Designer: Laura Polzin

Cataloging-in-Publication Data
Names: MacCarald, Clara, author.
Title: Becoming an American citizen / by Clara MacCarald.
Description: Minneapolis, MN : Abdo Publishing, [2017] | Series: American
    citizenship | Includes bibliographical references and index.
Identifiers: LCCN 2015960488 | ISBN 9781680782400 (lib. bdg.) |
    ISBN 9781680776515 (ebook)
Subjects: LCSH: Citizenship--United States--Juvenile literature. | Naturalization-
    -United States--Juvenile literature. | Americanization--United States--
    Juvenile literature.
Classification: DDC 323.6--dc23
LC record available at http://lccn.loc.gov/2015960488

CONTENTS

CHAPTER ONE

WHO IS A US CITIZEN?

A citizen is a legal member of a nation or country. In the United States, people become citizens by birth or by law. Any person born within the United States or its territories is a citizen. Children born abroad to a US parent or parents are citizens too. Other people must apply to become US citizens. They go through

The Statue of Liberty on Liberty Island in New York Harbor

A passport control entry gate for non-US citizens at a San Francisco, California, airport

a process called naturalization. A person must meet certain requirements to naturalize.

All US citizens are equal under the law regardless of how a person became a citizen. Natural-born citizens have one advantage. The US Constitution requires a president to be a "natural born Citizen."

Citizens of the United States have the right to vote. They have the right to fair trials. They enjoy the freedoms found in the Constitution. They have responsibilities too. The United States depends on its people. Citizens make up the government. They are called to serve on juries. They are also expected to defend the country.

Types of Noncitizens

Noncitizens living in the United States are legally called aliens. They cannot vote. They cannot hold public office at the federal level. They can be removed from the country. Aliens are removed from the United States every year for breaking the law.

Selective Service

Many young men were drafted into the US military in the past. The US government ended the draft in 1973. Today, the US military has an all-volunteer force. If a major war began and the draft started again, the Selective Service System would choose and evaluate men. Currently almost all men living in the United States who are 18 to 25 years old must register with the Selective Service. This includes undocumented immigrants and legal permanent residents. Citizens who do not register can be fined, jailed, or denied government benefits. Immigrants who are eligible but do not register cannot naturalize for five years.

Illegal Aliens

Alien might make you think of science fiction. Should the government continue using it as a word for noncitizens? US congressman Joaquin Castro doesn't think so. The Texas Democrat believes the word is offensive. He introduced a new bill in October 2015. The bill calls for the phrase *foreign national* to be used. *Illegal alien* would change to *undocumented foreign national.*

Most noncitizens need a visa to visit the United States. Different visas are available for different reasons. Foreigners attending a US school need a student visa. Other visitors might come for a vacation or for a job.

Certain visas allow noncitizens to live permanently in the United States. The government gives legal permanent residents a card. Years ago its color was green. This is why people still call the permanent resident card a green card. Family members or employers can sponsor an immigrant.

Millions of immigrants arrived in the United States at Ellis Island in New York in the late 1800s and early 1900s.

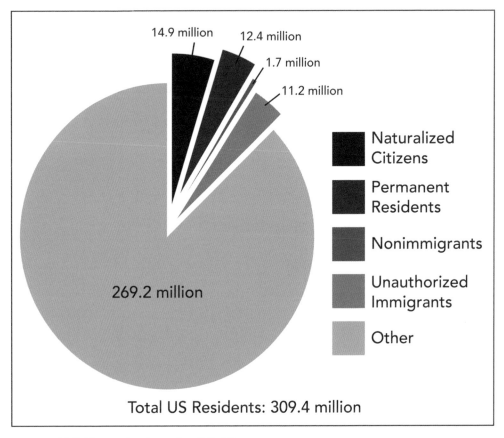

14.9 million

12.4 million

1.7 million

11.2 million

Naturalized Citizens

Permanent Residents

Nonimmigrants

Unauthorized Immigrants

Other

269.2 million

Total US Residents: 309.4 million

US Population in 2010
This pie chart shows the number of people living in the United States in 2010. The number of unauthorized immigrants comes from one study. Other studies have found different numbers. Why might it be hard to count unauthorized immigrants? Would you expect these numbers to change from year to year?

Some aliens live in the United States without the permission of the government. They may have not applied for a visa. Or they may have stayed after one expired. Some people call them illegal immigrants.

This is because their presence in the country is against the law. They are also called unauthorized or undocumented. Being in the United States illegally makes it harder to get a green card.

The United States is often called a nation of immigrants. Nearly 72 million people from 206 countries have settled in the United States since its founding in 1776. The way immigrants become naturalized has changed over time. The issue of who gets to claim American citizenship is often up for debate. The United States continues to attract people from around the world. Each year, more than half a million people become new citizens.

CHAPTER TWO

THE FOURTEENTH AMENDMENT

Almost anyone born on US soil is a US citizen. It doesn't matter if a child's parents are noncitizens. A right to citizenship at birth is called birthright citizenship. The Fourteenth Amendment sets down the rules for birthright citizenship in the United States.

The Fourteenth Amendment was written after the American Civil War (1861–1865). The war led to

This Union soldier and his family became US citizens after the country ratified the Fourteenth Amendment in 1866.

Native Americans

Native Americans have been born on US soil for longer than anyone. Yet most were not citizens of the United States. They lived in their own sovereign nations. The Citizenship Clause did not cover them. The Supreme Court upheld this in *Elk v. Wilkins* in 1884. John Elk had left his Winnebago nation. In 1880, he tried to vote in Nebraska. Judges ruled that Elk was not a citizen. In their opinion, he had not been born under US rule. He would have to apply for US citizenship. Only in 1924 were all American Indians made US citizens.

the ending of slavery in the United States. The amendment's writers were more concerned with the status of former slaves than with immigrants. Were freed slaves citizens? A Supreme Court decision from before the war said no. The case was *Dred Scott v. Sandford*. The judges said that black people were not and could never be US citizens. It did not matter if they were free or slaves.

Southern states passed "Black Codes" after the war. These laws limited the rights of former slaves. Some members of Congress wanted to protect the freed slaves. Congress proposed the Fourteenth Amendment to the Constitution. It guaranteed the rights of former slaves. It was ratified in 1868. The first sentence is called the Citizenship Clause. It states that all people born or naturalized in the United States and subject to its laws are US citizens. The amendment also barred states from limiting the rights of citizens.

Banning the Chinese

Immigration was a big topic in the late nineteenth century. Some Americans wanted to limit Chinese immigration to the United States. Many had racist attitudes against Chinese immigrants, and they worried the Chinese would take their jobs. Congress passed a Chinese Exclusion Act in 1882 that banned the immigration of Chinese laborers for ten years. Those already in the country could not bring in their wives or children. They also could not become citizens. But some had US-born children.

One such child was Wong Kim Ark. He was born in San Francisco, California. He saw himself as a US

The Opposing View

Chief Justice Melville Fuller did not agree that Wong Kim Ark was a citizen. He wrote the opposing view. Fuller cited earlier Supreme Court decisions. These found the Citizenship Clause did not apply to the children of visitors. The children of people on the path to being citizens might be covered. But Chinese immigrants were barred from naturalizing by both China and the United States. For these reasons, Fuller wrote that the Chinese could never be US citizens. The clause could not give them citizenship.

citizen. In 1895, he tried to return from a trip to China. A US official stopped him. The official said he was a Chinese citizen. His case reached the Supreme Court as *United States v. Wong Kim Ark*. The justices needed to interpret the Fourteenth Amendment. In 1898, six of eight justices agreed that birthright citizenship applied to the children of immigrants. Wong was a citizen.

Wong Kim Ark paved the way for generations of new US citizens. The following passage on his life is by Erika Lee. Lee is the director of the Immigration History Research Center in Minnesota:

> Despite his history-making case, [Wong Kim Ark] reaped little benefit. His citizenship and legal status were never fully recognized by the U.S. government, and he remained an outsider in the land of his birth. Like all Chinese in America, Wong was required to carry a "Certificate of Identity" at all times to verify his status as a legal resident. Whenever he entered or re-entered the country, Wong also had to laboriously fill out forms and be interrogated about his right to return to the land of his birth.

Source: Erika Lee. "A History Lesson for Donald Trump and His Supporters." New York Daily News. *New York Daily News*, August 18, 2015. Web. Accessed December 7, 2015.

Back It Up

The author of this passage is using evidence to support a point. Write a paragraph describing the point the author is making. Then write down two or three pieces of evidence the author uses to make the point.

CHAPTER THREE

BIRTHRIGHT CITIZENSHIP

Birthright citizenship is not unique to the United States. Almost all North and South American countries currently grant automatic citizenship to children born to illegal aliens. In the United States, many people have used this path to citizenship and contributed to the country over the past 150 years.

Anyone born in the United States, regardless of where his or her parents come from, is a US citizen.

Dual Citizenship

Do people always know what country they belong to? Birthright citizenship can make it tricky. Senator Ted Cruz of Texas discovered this as an adult. He had both American and Canadian citizenship. He had been born in Calgary, Canada. His mother was a US citizen at the time of his birth. Cruz said he thought he had to claim his Canadian citizenship. Instead, it was granted automatically. Cruz formally gave up his Canadian citizenship in 2013.

But only 30 of the world's 194 countries currently grant birthright citizenship. No countries in Europe or East Asia do. Australia had birthright citizenship, but in 2007 it became the most recent country to end the policy.

Some Americans think it is wrong to grant birthright citizenship to unauthorized immigrants. They see it as a reward for illegal behavior. They sometimes call children born to noncitizens in the United States *anchor babies*. The child could anchor the family to the United States. The situation might make it less likely for the parents to be removed from the United States.

Donald Trump pledged to strip babies born to undocumented immigrants of their birthright citizenship if he were elected president.

Change the Law?

The year 2015 was the year before a US presidential

election. Many candidates wanted their parties'

PERSPECTIVES

A Law Problem?

People entering the United States illegally are a big problem. Or are they? Kurt Eichenwald doesn't think so. He wrote an article in *Newsweek* in October of 2015. He cited studies. Some suggested unauthorized immigrants might commit fewer crimes than citizens. Others found they create some jobs. Many unauthorized immigrants pay federal and state taxes. Eichenwald wrote that arresting and jailing illegal immigrants is expensive. Many people want entry into the United States. He wrote that immigration laws are the problem. He believes the United States needs more ways for people to enter legally.

nomination. Some Republican candidates spoke against birthright citizenship. Several didn't think it should apply to the children of unauthorized immigrants.

Could lawmakers end the practice in the United States? Congress could make a new law. People against immigration have tried this in the past. More than one-half of the US public opposes changing the Constitution to end birthright citizenship.

In *Plyler v. Doe* (1982), the Supreme Court decided that the Fourteenth Amendment protected unauthorized immigrants. Justice William Brennan explains the court's reasons for the opinion:

> Appellants argue at the outset that undocumented aliens, because of their immigration status, are not "persons within the jurisdiction" of the State of Texas, and that they therefore have no right to the equal protection of Texas law. We reject this argument. Whatever his status under the immigration laws, an alien is surely a "person" in any ordinary sense of that term. Aliens, even aliens whose presence in this country is unlawful, have long been recognized as "persons" guaranteed due process of law by the Fifth and Fourteenth Amendments. . . . Indeed, we have clearly held that the Fifth Amendment protects aliens whose presence in this country is unlawful from invidious discrimination by the Federal Government.

Source: "Plyler v. Doe." Legal Information Institute. *Cornell University Law School, 1982. Web. Accessed March 9, 2016.*

Consider Your Audience

Review this passage closely. Adapt this passage for your school principal or friends. Write a blog post about it for the new audience. Write it so they can understand it. How does your new approach differ from the original text and why?

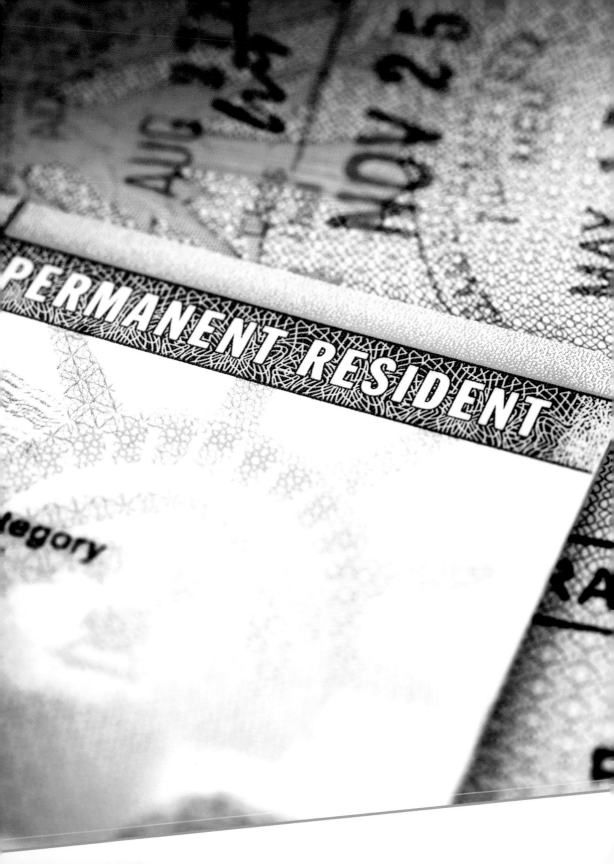

RULES FOR NATURALIZING

Not everyone can become a US citizen. Only certain people are eligible for this process, which is called naturalization. People must be at least 18 years old to apply for themselves. Children need a parent's help. Children can also become US citizens if they are adopted.

Almost all candidates start as immigrants. Before applying for citizenship, they must have been

A permanent resident card

Children Become Citizens

Children can naturalize when their parents do. But certain conditions must be met. They must be permanent residents of the United States. They must be living with their parent or parents. Foreign children adopted by US citizens also automatically become citizens. Children who meet these requirements need not apply for citizenship. They do need to apply for proof that they are a citizen.

permanent residents for several years. The general requirement is five years. Candidates must have been present on US soil for at least 30 months of that time. They can travel out of the country. But each trip must last less than six months. They need to have lived in their current state for three months.

There are many special situations. Only three years of permanent residence are required for a person who is married to a US citizen. For foreign employees of the US government abroad, time working overseas counts as time in the United States.

Other Requirements

Applicants must have a good moral character. How do immigration officials know? They can look at a person's criminal record. Candidates must be honest about their criminal record. If officials discover lies in the application, they can deny the application. They can even take away citizenship later.

Not all offenses keep people from gaining citizenship. In most cases, officials only consider crimes committed in the

PERSPECTIVES
Who Should Become a US Citizen?

Congress passed the first US naturalization law in 1790. It tightly restricted citizenship. It limited eligibility to "free white people." Other requirements were similar to today's. Applicants must have resided in the United States for two years. They needed to be "a person of good character." In 1798, Congress passed a law that required immigrants to live in the United States for 14 years before becoming eligible for citizenship. In 1802, the residency requirement was reduced to five years.

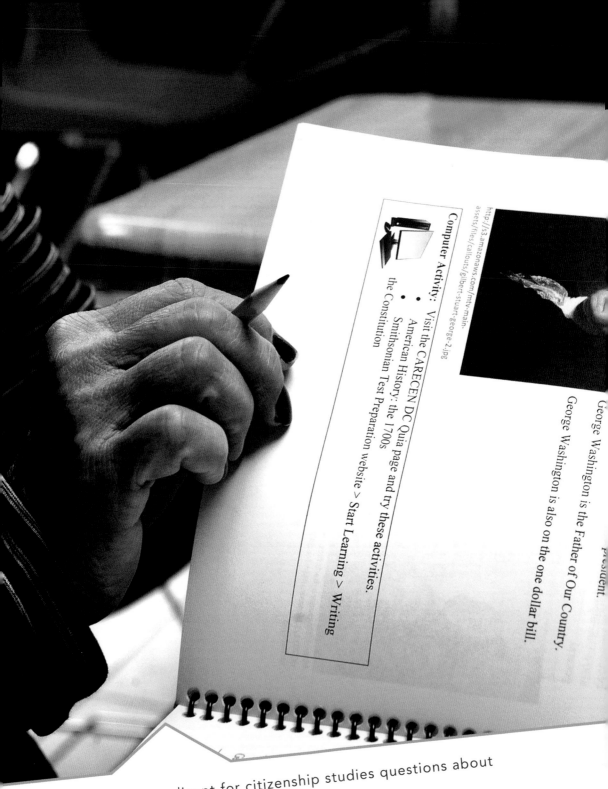

President.

George Washington is the Father of Our Country.

George Washington is also on the one dollar bill.

http://s3.amazonaws.com/mtv-main-
assets/files/callouts/gilbert-stuart-george-2.jpg

Computer Activity:

- Visit the CARECEN DC Quia page and try these activities.
- American History: the 1700s
- Smithsonian Test Preparation website > Start Learning > Writing the Constitution

An applicant for citizenship studies questions about American history.

past five years. Some offenses matter for longer. A person convicted of murder can never become a naturalized US citizen.

Candidates must actively support the US Constitution. They cannot have been part of a communist or terrorist group. They must be willing to say the Oath of Allegiance to the United States. They need a basic command of the English language. They must know about US history and government. All of these are basic requirements of the application process.

FURTHER EVIDENCE

Chapter Four covers who is eligible for US citizenship. What was one of the main points of this chapter? What evidence supports this point? The website at the link below also covers the requirements for naturalizing. Find a quote from the website that supports the main point that you identified.

Learn about Naturalization
mycorelibrary.com/american-citizen

APPLYING TO NATURALIZE

A candidate for US citizenship begins by filling out Form N-400. This is the application for citizenship. Its 21 pages contain questions about the candidate's eligibility. There are questions about one's family and criminal record. Some questions ask about residency. Other questions ask about jobs.

A Colombian immigrant studies ahead of her citizenship exam in New York City.

Some answers may require supporting material. For example, an applicant might have an excuse for being arrested. They may not have been charged with any crime. Candidates must prove other things. They must include papers to prove a legal name change. The spouse of a US citizen needs to include a marriage certificate and other records.

All paperwork must be sent to the US Citizenship and Immigration Services (USCIS). Permanent residents send a copy of their green card. The packet should

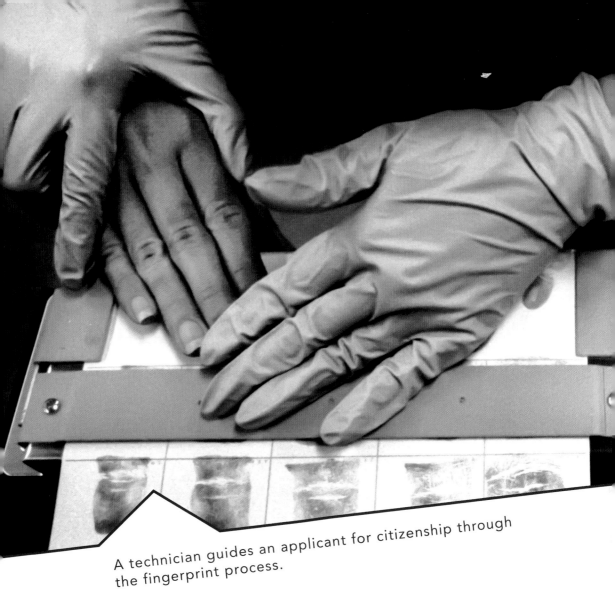

A technician guides an applicant for citizenship through the fingerprint process.

include two color photos of the applicant. The process requires two fees. One fee covers the application. The other pays for fingerprinting. The USCIS uses fingerprints and other information to run a background check.

Test Waivers

Some tests are waived for some applicants. The option is available to older people. English is not required for people older than 50 who have been immigrants for 20 years. They can test in the language of their choice. At age 55, the requirement drops to 15 years. Special consideration is given to people age 65 or older when taking the civics test. An easier civics test is available, if they have been a legal resident for 20 years. Testing can be hard for people with disabilities too. They can request to skip the tests altogether. Otherwise their tests can be altered.

The Interview

USCIS reviews every application. Then an interview is scheduled. Applicants can prepare with online resources and classes. At the interview, a USCIS officer will ask about details from the form. An officer will also give the English and civics tests.

The examiner asks questions in English. A person's responses show his or her ability to understand and speak in English. They must also read out loud one of three sentences. They must write one of three sentences correctly. Some applicants qualify for easier tests.

The civics test is also given out loud. The examiner asks up to ten questions. These are drawn from a list of 100. The test covers US government, principles of the US Constitution, and history. Other topics include holidays and symbols. Six correct answers are required to pass.

EXPLORE ONLINE

Chapter Five talks about the civics test. The website below has the 100 questions on the test. The test covers US government, US history, and more general civics. Read through a few questions in each section. Are you surprised by any of them? Do you think most citizens would know the answers?

Civics (History and Government) Questions for the Naturalization Test

mycorelibrary.com/american-citizen

The Declaration of
Independence
and the
Constitution
of the United States

...zenship
... ...migration

CHAPTER SIX

BECOMING A US CITIZEN

After the interview, the USCIS reviews the applicant's case for citizenship. The USCIS has 120 days to make a decision. The USCIS officer might decide at the interview. Otherwise they send a letter to the applicant. The case may be put on hold, denied, or approved.

An applicant gets another chance if he or she fails one of the tests. A new interview is scheduled.

An immigrant waits to become a US citizen.

Soldiers from different branches of the military take the Oath of Allegiance in New York.

Some cases are put on hold because of incomplete information. The applicant has 30 days to correct this or the application is denied. Failing tests for a second time also leads to denial.

A case is denied when the USCIS determines an applicant is not eligible. If an applicant is approved, he or she will receive a letter about three to six weeks later. The letter will tell the applicant the time and place of their oath ceremony.

Taking the Oath

Saying the Oath of Allegiance is the final step in becoming a citizen. Some oath ceremonies involve hundreds of people. They might be held at a significant place,

PERSPECTIVES
Split Loyalties?

New citizens swear loyalty to the United States. They also promise to give up other ties. But some people remain citizens of their home countries. This is called dual citizenship. Journalist Jorge Ramos is a Mexican citizen. In 2008 he became a US citizen too. Ramos has two passports. He votes in elections in both countries. He says he is proud to have dual citizenship.

Modifying the Oath

The oath is at the center of citizenship ceremonies. But not everyone says the same words. Some say none at all. People unable to understand or say the oath due to medical reasons are excused. The oath may also be modified for someone's religious beliefs. People can leave out, "so help me God." If new citizens are opposed to war, they can avoid promises to bear arms or otherwise support the military. They must prove their beliefs are "sincere, meaningful, and deeply held."

such as a national park. They may be scheduled for a national holiday. Every year, approximately 680,000 people are naturalized in the United States.

At the ceremony, new citizens turn in their green cards. They must answer questions about the time since their interview. Did anything happen that might affect their eligibility? Often, guest speakers and music are part of the ceremony. At long last, the applicants say the oath. They swear to renounce loyalty to foreign leaders and states. They promise to support and defend the Constitution and US laws.

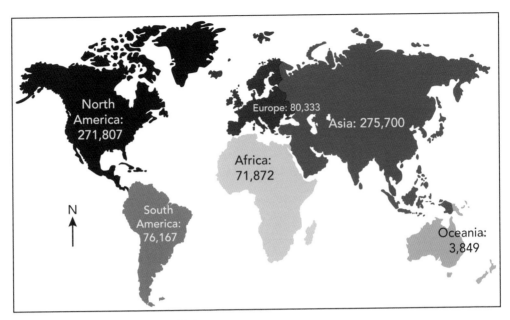

Origins of New US Citizens

This map shows the origin of people naturalizing as US citizens in 2013. What do you notice about the different regions? How might it relate to the immigration debates from Chapter Three?

Finally, the applicant is a US citizen. They receive their Certificate of Naturalization. They get a "US Citizenship Welcome Packet." They become part of a tradition stretching back more than 200 years. They join millions of US citizens protected by the US Constitution.

- People can be born US citizens or they can naturalize.
- Legal permanent residents have an identification called a green card.
- Unauthorized immigrants do not have permission to be in the United States.
- The Fourteenth Amendment grants birthright citizenship to people born in the United States.
- The Fourteenth Amendment protected the rights of former slaves.
- In 1898, the Supreme Court found birthright citizenship applies to the children of immigrants.
- Birthright citizenship now applies to the children of unauthorized immigrants born on US soil.
- Some people think birthright citizenship rewards illegal behavior.
- People argue the laws should be applied differently or changed.
- There are requirements to naturalize as a US citizen.

- Most green card holders can apply for naturalization after five years.
- Children must have a parent naturalize.
- Form N-400 is the application for citizenship.
- Applicants must attend an interview and pass an English and civics test.
- After passing, applicants attend an oath ceremony.
- Taking the Oath of Allegiance is the last step in becoming a US citizen.

STOP AND THINK

Say What?

Studying citizenship and amendments can mean learning a lot of new vocabulary. Find five words in this book you've never heard before. Use a dictionary to find out what they mean. Then write the meanings in your own words and use each word in a new sentence.

Another View

Chapter Two talks about how and why the Fourteenth Amendment came about. As you know, every source is different. Ask a librarian or another adult to help you find another source about this event. Write a short essay comparing and contrasting the new source's point of view with that of this book's author. What is the point of view of each author? How are they similar and why? How are they different and why?

Why Do I Care?

Maybe you have no plans to change your citizenship. But that doesn't mean naturalization is unimportant to you. Do you have friends or family who have naturalized in the United States? How might your life be different if you were an immigrant in the United States who wanted to become a citizen?

Surprise Me

Chapter Four discusses who is eligible for citizenship. After reading this book, what two or three facts about who can apply to naturalize did you find most surprising? Write a few sentences about each fact. Why did you find each fact surprising?

GLOSSARY

alien
a legal term for a noncitizen

allegiance
loyalty

amendment
a formal change to a bill or constitution

birthright
a right granted automatically at birth

civics
the study of government and citizenship

eligible
meeting the requirements

immigrant
a person who has moved to a foreign country

jurisdiction
legal power over someone or something

naturalize
to become a citizen after birth

ratify
to formally approve

undocumented
not recorded

waive
give permission not to do something

LEARN MORE

Books

Kimmel, Barbara Brooks, and Alan M. Lubiner. *Citizenship Made Simple: An Easy-to-Read Guide to the U.S. Citizenship Process – 4th Edition.* Chester, NJ: Next Decade, 2006.

Latta, Susan M. *The Reconstruction Era.* Minneapolis, MN: Abdo Publishing Company, 2014.

Websites

To learn more about American Citizenship, visit **booklinks.abdopublishing.com**. These links are routinely monitored and updated to provide the most current information available.

Visit **mycorelibrary.com** for free additional tools for teachers and students.

INDEX

ABOUT THE AUTHOR

Clara MacCarald is a writer from central New York with a master's degree in biology. She has written many articles about science and local news for community newspapers.